Learn CHINESE (Mandarin) Through Fairy Tales

S0-BNS-547

Cinderella

Book Design & Production: Slangman Kids *(a division of Slangman Inc. and Slangman Publishing)*

Copy Editor: Julie Bobrick
Illustrated by: "Migs!" Sandoval
Translators: Li Li Peters & Ming Tao
Proofreaders: Lin Zhu & Connie Sun

Copyright © 2006 by David Burke

Published by: Slangman Kids *(a division of Slangman Inc. and Slangman Publishing)* 12206 Hillslope Street, Studio City, CA 91604 •USA • Toll Free Telephone from USA: 1-877-SLANGMAN (1-877-752-6462) • From outside the USA: 1-818-SLANGMAN (1-818-752-6462) • Worldwide Fax 1-413-647-1589 • Email: info@slangman.com • Website: www.slangman.com

Slangman is a trademark of David Burke. All rights reserved. Reproduction or translation of any part of this work beyond that permitted by section 107 or 108 of the 1976 United States Copyright Act without the permission of the copyright owner is unlawful. Requests for permission or further information should be addressed to the Permissions Department, Slangman Publishing. This publication is designed to provide accurate and authoritative information in regard to the subject matter covered. The persons, entities and events in this book are fictitious. Any similarities with actual persons or entities, past and present, are purely coincidental.

"Migs!" Sandoval

our illustrator

Miguel *"Migs!"* Sandoval has been drawing cartoons since the age of 6 and has worked on numerous national commercials and movies as a sculptor, model builder, and illustrator. He was born in Los Angeles and was raised in a bilingual household, speaking English and Spanish. He currently lives in San Francisco where he is working on his new comic book series!

ISBN10: 1891888-79X
ISBN13: 978189888-793
Printed in the U.S.A.

10 9 8 7 6 5 4 3 2 1

Order Form

Preview chapters & shop online!

www.slangman.com

SHIP TO: ______________________________

____

____

____

Contact/Phone/Email: ______________________________

SHIPPING

Domestic Orders

SURFACE MAIL
(Delivery time 5-7 business days).
Add $5 shipping/handling for the first item, $1.50 for each additional item.

RUSH SERVICE
Available at extra charge. Contact us for details.

International Orders

SURFACE MAIL
(Delivery time 6-8 weeks).
Add $6 shipping/handling for the first item, $2 for each additional item. Note that shipping to some countries may be more expensive. Contact us for details.

AIRMAIL (approx. 3-5 business days)
Available at extra charge. Contact us for details.

Method of Payment (Check one):

☐ Personal Check or Money Order
(Must be in U.S. funds and drawn on a U.S. bank.)

☐ VISA ☐ Master Card ☐ Discover ☐ American Express ☐ JCB

Credit Card Number

Signature

Expiration Date

QTY	ISBN-13	TITLE	PRICE	LEVEL	TOTAL COST
		English to CHINESE (Mandarin)			
	9781891888-793	**Cinderella**	$14.95	1	
	9781891888-854	**Goldilocks**	$14.95	2	
	9781891888-915	**Beauty and the Beast**	$14.95	3	
		English to FRENCH			
	9781891888-755	**Cinderella**	$14.95	1	
	9781891888-816	**Goldilocks**	$14.95	2	
	9781891888-878	**Beauty and the Beast**	$14.95	3	
		English to GERMAN			
	9781891888-762	**Cinderella**	$14.95	1	
	9781891888-830	**Goldilocks**	$14.95	2	
	9781891888-885	**Beauty and the Beast**	$14.95	3	
		English to HEBREW			
	9781891888-922	**Cinderella**	$14.95	1	
	9781891888-939	**Goldilocks**	$14.95	2	
	9781891888-946	**Beauty and the Beast**	$14.95	3	
		English to ITALIAN			
	9781891888-779	**Cinderella**	$14.95	1	
	9781891888-823	**Goldilocks**	$14.95	2	
	9781891888-892	**Beauty and the Beast**	$14.95	3	
		English to JAPANESE			
	9781891888-786	**Cinderella**	$14.95	1	
	9781891888-847	**Goldilocks**	$14.95	2	
	9781891888-908	**Beauty and the Beast**	$14.95	3	
		English to SPANISH			
	9781891888-748	**Cinderella**	$14.95	1	
	9781891888-809	**Goldilocks**	$14.95	2	
	9781891888-861	**Beauty and the Beast**	$14.95	3	
Japanese to ENGLISH		絵本で えいご を学ぼう			
	9781891888-038	**Cinderella**	$14.95	1	
	9781891888-045	**Goldilocks**	$14.95	2	
	9781891888-052	**Beauty and the Beast**	$14.95	3	
Korean to ENGLISH		동화를 통한 **ENGLISH** 배우기			
	9781891888-076	**Cinderella**	$14.95	1	
	9781891888-106	**Goldilocks**	$14.95	2	
	9781891888-113	**Beauty and the Beast**	$14.95	3	
Spanish to ENGLISH		Aprende **INGLÉS** con cuentos de hadas			
	9781891888-953	**Cinderella**	$14.95	1	
	9781891888-960	**Goldilocks**	$14.95	2	
	9781891888-977	**Beauty and the Beast**	$14.95	3	

Total for Merchandise	
Sales Tax *(California residents only add applicable sales tax)*	
Shipping *(See left)*	
ORDER GRAND TOTAL	

Prices subject to change

SLANGMAN® KIDS
(a division of Slangman Publishing)

**** TO PLACE AN ORDER - CALL, FAX, OR EMAIL: ****
Phone: 1-818-752-6462 • Fax: 1-413-647-1589
Email: info@slangman.com • Web: www.slangman.com
12206 Hillslope Street • Studio City, CA 91604

(FORM 071606

Dedication

The entire "Foreign Language Through Fairy Tales" series is dedicated to all the children of the world.

It is through their understanding, appreciation, and celebration of our differences that the world will become a better and safer place for us all.

1

nuhaizi
(女孩子)
piaoliang
(漂亮)
fangzi
(房子)

Once upon a time, there lived a poor girl named Cinderella who was very pretty. The **nuhaizi**, who was very **piaoliang**, lived in a small house with her stepmother and two

2

stepsisters. At times it was difficult for the poor **nuhaizi** to live in such a small **fangzi** with her stepmother and two stepsisters. Why? Because they were

jealous that she was so **piaoliang** which is why her stepmother was extra mean to her. But the poor **nuhaizi** never complained about living in a small

huai
(坏)

fangzi with her stepmother, who was very **huai**, and two stepsisters, even though they forced her to do all the work in the entire **fangzi** day in and day out!

5

Royal Invitation
Who: The King
What: A Royal Ball
Where: The Castle
When: This Saturday, 8pm
Why: To find a wife for the prince
Valet parking available

wuhui (舞会)
da (大)

One day, a royal invitation arrived at the **fangzi** of the poor **nuhaizi**. The king was throwing a party for the prince. And the **wuhui** was going to be big. The **wuhui**

was going to be *very* **da**! The prince was handsome, not only **yingjun**, but also kind. Every **nuhaizi** in the land was invited to the **wuhui**, so that he could choose a wife.

yingjun
(英俊)

qizi
(妻子)

7

wangzi
(王子)

The king and queen also hoped the prince would find a **qizi** who was truly **piaoliang** both inside and out. The **wangzi** was very excited about his royal **wuhui**!

8

The night of the **wuhui** for the **wangzi** arrived but Cinderella was very sad. Her stepmother was so **huai**, she wouldn't let her leave the **fanzi** to go to the **wuhui**.

shangxin
(伤心)

9

She was so **shangxin**, she started to cry. She was the only **nuhaizi** not allowed to leave her **fangzi** and get the chance to meet the **wangzi** at the **wuhui** and become his **qizi**.

Suddenly a voice from behind her said, "My dear, I'm your fairy godmother and you'll be able to go to the **wuhui** of the **wangzi** and... you'll be wearing an elegant dress!"

qunzi
(裙子)

11

And with a wave of her wand, Cinderella was now wearing the most elegant **qunzi** imaginable. "Thank you! **Xiexie ni**!" exclaimed Cinderella. She was now a

Xiexie ni
(谢谢你)

nuhaizi who was truly **piaoliang**, wearing an elegant **qunzi**, and eager to leave her **fangzi** to meet the **wangzi** at the **wuhui**, and maybe, just maybe become his **qizi**.

13

wuye
(午夜)

"One moment!" the fairy godmother added. "Make sure to leave the **wuhui** by midnight because your **qunzi** will change back to the way it was!"

14

Cinderella thought for a moment and then said, "I'll remember to leave before **wuye**." So the **nuhaizi**, who was very **piaoliang**, left for the **wuhui**. She was

15

gaoxing
(高兴)

no longer **shangxin**, but very happy to be meeting the **wangzi**. As she got out of her carriage, she could hear the **wuhui** and indeed it was **da**! Cinderella walked in

and wasn't too **gaoxing** to see more than one **nuhaizi** waiting to meet the **wangzi**. But after a moment, she calmed down and was ready to

17

meet the **wangzi** face to face. And indeed he was very **yingjun**! She couldn't believe her eyes! And clearly the **wangzi** never saw a **nuhaizi** more **piaoliang** in his life!

18

"**Xiexie ni** very much for inviting me to your **wuhui**," said Cinderella. "You're welcome! **Buyong keqi**!" said the **wangzi**. Cinderella and the **wangzi**

Buyong keqi
(不用客气)

19

danced and danced for hours, until the stroke of **wuye** was finally upon them which the **nuhaizi** had completely forgotten about! Poof! Her **qunzi** vanished!

20

"Goodbye!" shouted Cinderella. "**Zaijian**! And **xiexie ni** for inviting me!" "**Buyong keqi**," responded the **wangzi**. And Cinderella ran back to her **fangzi**.

Zaijian
(再见)

21

xiezi
(鞋子)

The only thing she left behind was a glass shoe. The **wangzi** was extremely **shangxin** and went from town to town looking for a **nuhaizi** whose

22

foot would fit the glass **xiezi**.
After days of eliminating **nuhaizi** after **nuhaizi**, the **wangzi** was more **shangxin** than ever, but he

jiao
(脚)

23

had one more **fangzi** to visit. The **huai** stepmother and stepsisters ran out to try on the glass **xiezi**, but it was no use. He still couldn't find a **jiao** to match the **xiezi**.

The **wangzi** was **shangxin** and about to give up, but at that very moment, he spotted Cinderella. There was something very special about her, aside from being so **piaoliang**.

25

He just had to see if her **jiao** was the one that could fit the glass **xiezi**. He knelt down in front of the **nuhaizi** and slid the **xiezi** on her **jiao**.

And her **jiao** did fit the glass **xiezi** perfectly! Suddenly in a puff of smoke, Cinderella's fairy godmother reappeared and changed her back into the same

nuhaizi in the elegant **qunzi** the **wangzi** had met at his **wuhui**. The **wangzi** was so very **gaoxing**! And Cinderella was especially **gaoxing** that she lost her glass

xiezi at the **wuhui** or the **wangzi** may never have found her – a **nuhaizi** as **piaoliang** on the inside as on the out! Soon, she became his **qizi** at a wedding that was far from

far from small. In fact, it was truly **da**! She was so very **gaoxing**. She would never, ever be **shangxin** again. And the **wangzi** and Cinderella lived in the castle happily ever after.